Story-Writing-Coding

with the

WeeBee engine

Published by
Crossbridge Books, Worcester
www.crossbridgeeducational.com
Copyright © Crossbridge Books 2020

Illustrations and weebee concept© R M Price-Mohr
Original weebee concept art by Rolf Mohr
Creator of the WeeBee engine C B Price

ISBN 978-1-8380028-1-7

†† CROSSBRIDGE BOOKS

Story-Writing-Coding

with the

WeeBee engine

by

Dr Colin Price

CONTENTS

		Page
Introduction and Overview		1
Chapter 1	Exploring some Code	4
Chapter 2	Assembling your Scene	7
Chapter 3	Character Movement - *Movement 'at'*	13
Chapter 4	Character Movement - *Movement 'to'*	17
Chapter 5	Coding two Characters	23
Chapter 6	Talking, Thinking, and Feeling	33
Chapter 7	Working with Props	40
Chapter 8	Some Simple Stories - *children's examples*	44
Chapter 9	Scene Management	51
Chapter 10	Adding your own Assets	54
Chapter 11	Working with Sound	60
Chapter 12	Story Types and Starters	63
Chapter 13	Advanced Coding	72
Chapter 14	WeeBee Engine Assets	82
Chapter 15	What you will find in the next book	87
Section 16	Code Index	89

Introduction and Overview

What you will learn

Story-Writing-Coding

So what does this actually mean? Well the answer is quite simple really. You will learn how to create an animated story where you see characters moving around a scene all on your computer screen. All you need is the *WeeBee* engine and a PC.

You can access the engine and a Quick Start Guide which explains how to install and run the engine at the link below. Use the information in the section '**For Schools 2020+**'. There is a chart of Characters, Props, Scenery and Backgrounds that you may want to print.

Any future updates to the engine, or other supporting materials will be found here.

http://colin-price.wbs.uni.worc.ac.uk/WeeBeeCode/WBC_2020.htm

The Chapters

Here is a summary of what you will learn in each chapter. It may be useful when you need to remind yourself how to code something.

Chapter 1

Here you will create a scene, including a single character, and make the character move around.

Chapter 2

This is all about creating a very interesting scene. You will add scenery and a character, and learn how to make a character move in front of, or behind scenery.

Chapter 3
Here you will explore how to make a character move at one place, such as jumping or spinning.

Chapter 4
This chapter extends character movement. You will find out how to make your character move around your scene.

Chapter 5
Here you will be introduced to coding two characters. This is important for any story. It's probably the hardest of all the chapters in this book.

Chapter 6
All characters can talk, think and show their emotions. This is important for your stories, and you will learn how to do these things in this chapter.

Chapter 7
This chapter introduces 'props'. Like characters, props can move but they can't display emotions.

Chapter 8
Here you will be guided to write four short stories: a 'Night Scene', 'A camping Trip', 'Terror on the Moon', and 'A Jumping Game'. This will prepare you for coding your own stories.

Chapter 9
A story comprises several chapters or, in the case of our coded stories, several scenes. Here you will learn how to split your code into scenes, and how to change between several scenes.

Chapter 10
Here you will learn how to add your own scenery, backgrounds, and characters, into the engine. All you need to do is to create some images!

Chapter 11
Adding sound can really enhance a story. Here you will learn how to add sound effects, music, and narration.

Chapter 12
This chapter helps you to write your story. You are shown some different types of story, and also how to get started.

Chapter 13
Here you will learn about advanced coding, how to use repetition and selection code constructs.

Chapter 14
Here are all the assets and code statements used in the WeeBee engine.

Chapter 15
Here you will find what you can learn about in the next book about Turtle Graphics.

How to use the engine

Open up the engine folder and double left click on **RUN_ME.bat**. Then the following screens will appear, after you have clicked on run

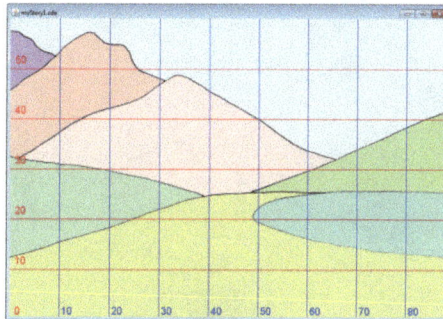

The box on the left is where you will type your code. On the right you see the 'canvas' where your animation will appear. There are two important buttons,

| Click to Run | Click to close-down |

1

Exploring some Code

Your first steps

Let's write a few lines of code to see what the 𝒲𝑒𝑒ℬ𝑒𝑒 engine can do. We'll add a big tree, the sun and then we'll add Pip. We'll get Pip to fly around exploring the scene.

Remember, whenever you see the blue icon ▶ which is the run-button, click on it in the toolbar, to make the animation run. After typing each line of code, press enter ↵ to create a new line for the next code statement.

Chapter 1 - Getting Started

Load	File > Open > chapter1.cde

1. Type the following code on line 11, to add a big tree at the place with coordinates 70,10

add(bigtree,70,10);

Then press enter

2. Type the following code on line 12, to add the sun in the sky.

add(sun,45,50);

Then press enter

3. Now let's add Pip by typing this on line 13.

add(pip,20,10);

Then press enter

4. Type these two lines of code. The first will make Pip rest a while and the second will make her fly up into the tree.

pip.rest();
pip.flyto(65,35);

Then press enter

5. Let's get Pip to fly down to the ground, and rest there a while. She is probably getting tired.

pip.flyto(55,12);
pip.rest();

6. Now let's get Pip to fly up to the top of the mountains, and look at the view.

```
pip.flyto3D(15,50);
pip.rest();
```

7. Finally, let's get Pip back to the meadow, where she can enjoy a well-deserved rest.

```
pip.flyto3D(10,10);
pip.rest();
```

| Save | It's important to save your code. **File > Save** |

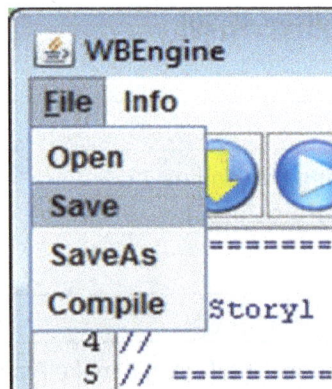

If you are going straight on to chapter two, you don't need to exit the Engine. Let's take a moment to think about what you have done. First you have written computer code to make a short animation. That is really fantastic isn't it? You know how to add scenery and a character to a scene, and make the character move around. Also, you probably made some errors and have learned to correct these and that makes you a real computer software programmer!

In the next chapter we shall think about how to create an interesting (and meaningful) scene. See you there!

2

Assembling your Scene

Scene Components

In this chapter you are going to assemble your own scene. You will need to choose:

* a background
* some scenery
* one character

It is important to choose elements that belong together. You will have a sheet with all of these things on.

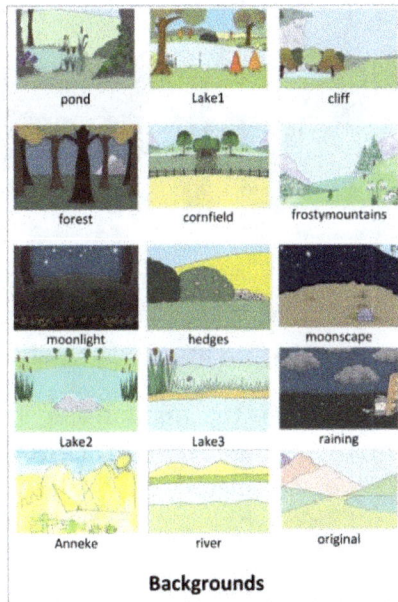

Backgrounds

Before you get going, look at the two examples below.

Here I started by choosing the background "Lake1". Notice that backgrounds have to be written in double quotes. You can see this on the left. Then I added a rush next to the rushes already in the background to create an area of rushes, shown on the right. Then I added a mushroom to the right because its colour was like the two bushes already there. I added the sun where it should be – in the sky! Finally I added some rocks at the bottom. I chose these since their colour would contrast with the green grass.

Here, on the left, I have chosen the "moonscape" background. Then I chose to add some more stars and some flying saucers. You can see these on the right. Two are placed on the ground to suggest a 'spaceport' and one in the sky which is probably coming in to land. The character I chose is Zon, who is clearly an alien. But I added two pieces of scenery which do not belong here. Can you find them?

Designing your Scene

Look at the sheet with backgrounds, scenery and characters. Choose a combination that works well together and makes sense, perhaps even suggesting a story. Start by choosing a background.

Load | **File > Open > chapter2a.cde**

1. Type the following code on line 11 to add your chosen background. I chose "moonscape".

```
setScene("moonscape");
```

2. Now add at least 5 or 6 items of scenery. Remember to choose them to create a scene that has meaning. Here's how I added the saucers in my example above.

```
add(saucer,20,10);
add(saucer,30,15);
add(saucer,60,40);
```

3. Now choose your character and add him or her to the scene. I chose Zon.

```
add(zon,50,15);
```

4. Now get your character to fly around, exploring the scene you created, like this.

```
zon.flyto(40,10);
zon.rest();
zon.flyto(20,50);
zon.rest();
```

Save | You don't need to exit if you are carrying on.

In-front or Behind?

Let's say we want to place a rock in front of a tree. How do we do this? The rule is very easy. It's to do with the *order* we add elements to the scene. The first thing you add is right at the back and the last thing you add is right at the front. So, if we need the rock in front of the tree, we first add the tree, and then we add the rock.

| Load | File > Open > chapter2b.cde | |

1. So let's try it out. Type the following code (starting on line 11) to add the big tree then the rock.

```
add(bigtree,40,0);
add(rock,40,0);
```

You will see that the rock is in front of the big tree.

How do we get characters to move in front of scenery or behind scenery? You will have noticed that they always move in front of the scenery. So how do we change this to get them moving behind the scenery?

We have to tell the piece of scenery to be located right at the front, using a different type of add command, like this:

```
add(bigtree,60,0,front);
```

2. Add the following code,

```
add(pip,10,0);
add(bigtree,60,0,front);
pip.flyto(80,0);
```

and you should find that Pip walks in front of the first tree, but behind the second.

3. Now add two more big trees, one at location (20,0) so that Pip will walk behind this tree, and one at location (75,0) so Pip will walk in-front of it. Now add code to get Pip to do this.

Save

Composing another Scene

In the next chapter we shall look at character movements in detail. But first let's create a scene to use in Chapter 3.

| Load | File > Open > chapter3a.cde | ▶ |

1. Choose a background and choose some scenery, and write code to compose your scene. ▶

2. Now add a bush at the front, so we can hide a character behind it. ▶

3. Now choose a character and place it so it appears behind the bush. Make sure you can just see a little bit of the character. You may need to tweak its coordinates. ▶

Save

3

Character Movement

Moving 'at'

Here we are going to look at actions that characters can perform at one place, such as jumping, spinning, getting larger and smaller, and other actions. We shall be using the scene you created at the end of the last chapter.

The code below will use the character Pip. You may have added a different one, like Mop. So you would need to type mop (or whichever character you have chosen) instead of pip in the code below.

 pip

 grog

 zon

 jig

 saff

 flup

 mop

 drax

 tod

Actions at a Place

If you exited the engine at the end of the last chapter, you will need to re-load chapter3a.

Load   **File > Open > chapter3a.cde**

1. Add the following lines of code and find out what they do.

```
pip.rest();
pip.jump();
pip.rest();
pip.jump(50);
```

2. Now replace the number 50 with a different number; you choose. This will help you find out what this number does. Try a few different numbers. Make sure you understand what this number does before you move on.

3. Let's move our character away from the bush and try some other actions. Add the following lines of code,

```
pip.flyto(50,10);
pip.rest();
pip.spin();
pip.rest();
pip.spin(10);
```

and experiment, changing the number 10 to other values. You should then understand what this number does.

4. Now add the following code to make your character walk left, then right, and left again. Notice how they flip direction.

```
pip.flyto(10,10);
pip.flipH();
pip.flyto(50,10);
pip.flipH();
pip.flyto(10,10);
```

5. Add the following lines of code and find out what they do

```
pip.rest();
pip.grow(1.5);
pip.rest();
pip.shrink(1.0);
```

6. And finally add these lines.

```
pip.hide();
pip.rest();
pip.show();
```

Save

Putting it all together

Load

File > Open > chapter3b.cde

1. Add some scenery to the cornfield scene; perhaps put one or two things 'at the front'.
2. Now add a character of your choice.
3. Make him/her move behind some scenery then jump.
4. Now make them hide and move them somewhere else.
5. Make them re-appear and then grow and grow.
6. Finally, return them to their normal size.

Save

4

Character Movement

Moving 'to'

In this chapter, we are going to investigate commands to make our character move from one place to another, the 'move-to' commands. You have already used one of these **pip.flyto(20,10);** but there are more. These move-to commands can be grouped like this:

<u>Group 1</u> takes two coordinates, X and Y, so the character can move to any place (X,Y) in the scene. For example, In the **flyto** command, Pip will fly to the location (30,20).

> **pip.flyto(30,20);**
> **pip.leapto(30,20);**
> **pip.flyto3D(70,55);**

<u>Group 2</u> takes a single coordinate X. That means the character will move in the x-direction only. That is, the horizontal direction, to the left or to the right. The **hopto** method does make the character fly up and down, but it lands at the same height it started.

> **pip.walkto(60);**
> **pip.runto(60);**
> **pip.hopto(60);**

<u>Group 3</u> also takes a single coordinate X, so the movement is in a horizontal direction, but here the legs or wings of the WeeBees move.

> **pip.stepto(60);**
> **flup.flapto(60);**

Here we are also going to begin to use the tab key when writing lines of code because this will become important at a later stage.

flyto, leapto, flyto3D

| Load | File > Open > chapter4a.cde | ▶ |

1. The scene has two barrels. Add these two lines of code to place Pip in front of the left barrel, and tell her to rest a while. (Remember to use the tab key to line up your lines of code before you type the code.)

add(pip,10,0);
pip.rest();

2. Now get Pip to fly to the second barrel, and rest there a while.

pip.flyto(75,17);
pip.rest();

3. Now get Pip to fly back to the first barrel and rest. You should be able to do this yourself. Please try, but if you get stuck, the answer can be found at the end of the chapter.

1

4. Now that Pip is back home, let's get her to **leapto** the second barrel and rest.

pip.leapto(75,17);
pip.rest();

5. Now get Pip to **leap** back to the first barrel and rest again. You should be able to do this yourself. Please try, but if you get stuck, the answer can be found at the end of the chapter.

2

6. Let's investigate moving with ***perspective,*** which means the character gets smaller when it moves into the distance. Pip is standing at the left barrel, and she has decided to move to a rock in the distance. As she moves into the distance, she appears smaller. Here's how we do it, add these lines of code.

pip.flyto3D(66,50);
pip.rest();

7. Now get Pip to get back to the first barrel using perspective. You should be able to do this yourself. Please try. But if you get stuck, the answer can be found at the end of the chapter.

3

Save

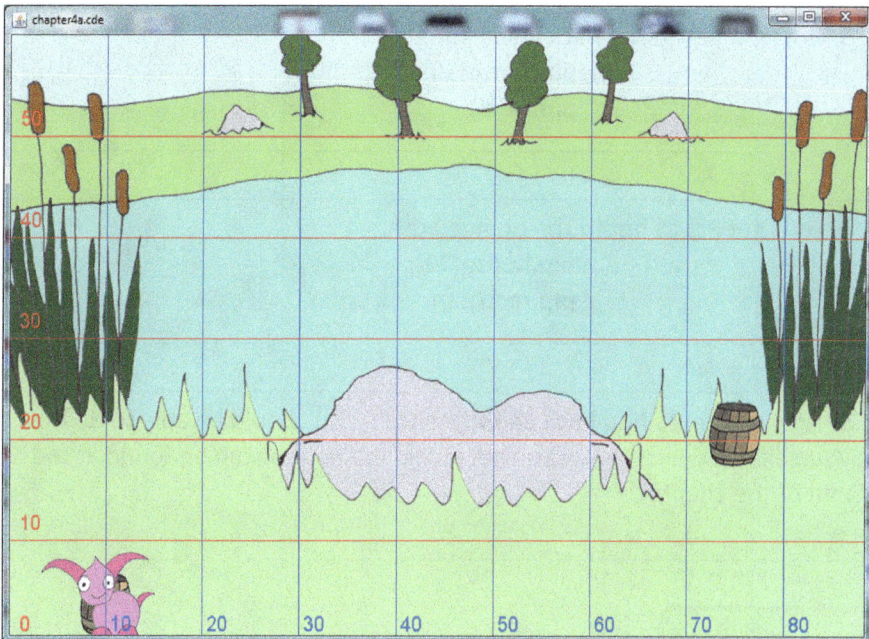

walkto, runto, hopto

| Load | File > Open > chapter4b.cde | ▶ |

1. Add this line of code to place Pip under the tree at the left, and tell her to rest a while.

add(pip,10,2);
pip.rest();

2. Now get Pip to walk to the orange bush which is located at X = 80.

pip.walkto(80);
pip.rest();

3. Now get her to run back under the tree.

pip.runto(10);
pip.rest();

4. Let's get Pip to **hopto** the orange bush.

pip.hopto(80);
pip.rest();

5. Now get Pip to **hop** back under the tree. You should be able to do this yourself. Please try, but if you get stuck, the answer can be found at the end of the chapter.

4

| Save |

stepto, flapto

Load   **File > Open > chapter4c.cde**   ▶

These commands give the characters some animation. The command **stepto** is used for WeeBees with legs and **flapto** for winged WeeBees.

1. Add Pip near the tree-trunk on the right, then after a while make her step to the tree-trunk on the left.

                     add(pip,80,2);
                     pip.rest();
                     pip.stepto(10);

2. Add Jig high up on the right, then after a while make her flap to the left.

                     add(jig,80,40);
                     jig.rest();
                     jig.flapto(10);

3. Now add Flup and Grog, and for each add three lines of code to get them to move across the scene.

4. Now find out what this code snippet does.

                     add(saff,110,40);
                     saff.rest();
                     saff.flapto(-20);

Save

So you see it's quite easy to get a character to fly across the scene. The value X = 110 puts Saff outside the scene to the right, then she flaps to X = -20 which is less than the left edge of the scene where we have X = 0.

Answers to Some questions

Here are the answers to the labelled questions (numbered yellow circles)

1. **pip.flyto(10,0);**
   pip.rest();

2. **pip.leapto(10,0);**
   pip.rest();

3. **pip.flyto3D(10,0);**

4. **pip.hopto(10);**

5

Coding two Characters

Synchronization

In this chapter we are going to learn how to code actions for two characters. When you have two characters they can both make an action at the same time, e.g. Pip will jump *and* Grog will spin. This is called *concurrent* behaviour. Or the characters can take turns in making actions, one after the other, e.g., Pip will jump *then* Pip will spin. This is called *sequential* behaviour. The key to coding these different behaviours lies in the use of the **rest();** method. Here are the four possible combinations of actions and rests for our two characters:

Code	pip.jump();
	grog.rest();
	
	pip.rest();
	grog.jump();
		pip.rest();
		grog.jump();
		
		pip.jump();
		grog.rest();
			pip.jump();
			grog.jump();
			
			pip.rest();
			grog.rest();
				pip.rest();
				grog.rest();
				
				pip.jump();
				grog.jump();

What happens	Pip jumps *then* Grog jumps.	Grog jumps *then* Pip jumps.	Pip and Grog jump together *then* they both rest.	Pip and Grog both rest a bit *then* they jump together.

You can see that each of the behaviours takes two lines of code for each character. The behaviour follows from where you put the rests. The guiding rule to writing code when you have two characters is simple.

*When you have two characters, you must write code in **pairs** of lines, one for each character.*

Two characters moving together

Load

File > Open > chapter5a.cde

The scene shows a river running through a meadow. There are hills in the distance. Make this more interesting by adding some scenery to the scene. Choose scenery that works well together, and choose good places to add your scenery.

1. Add Pip and Mop at the left side of your scene. Now let's get Pip to move close to the middle of the scene while Mop looks on. I will use **hopto** but you could choose other movement functions from Chapter 4.

```
pip.hopto(35);
mop.rest();
```

Then get Mop to move close to the middle of the scene while Pip looks on.

```
mop.hopto(45);
pip.rest();
```

2. Now get Pip to jump *then* Mop to jump. If you get stuck, the answer can be found at the end of the chapter.

1

3. Both characters rest a while then they jump together. Write the following code to do this.

```
pip.rest();
mop.rest();

pip.jump();
mop.jump();
```

4. Next Pip leaves the scene to the left while Mop looks on.

> **pip.flyto(-20,40);**
> **mop.rest();**

5. To end the action, write two lines of code to get mop to leave the scene to the right. If you get stuck, an answer can be found at the end of the chapter.

2

Save

A Scary Moment

Load

File > Open > chapter5b.cde

Here we are going to tell a little story. Pip is playing in the meadow, then the scary dragon Drax flies over her. Pip is scared so she runs and hides *behind* a bush.

1. Add Pip to the left of the scene, and add two bushes so that Pip can hide *behind* them later. Your scene should look like this.

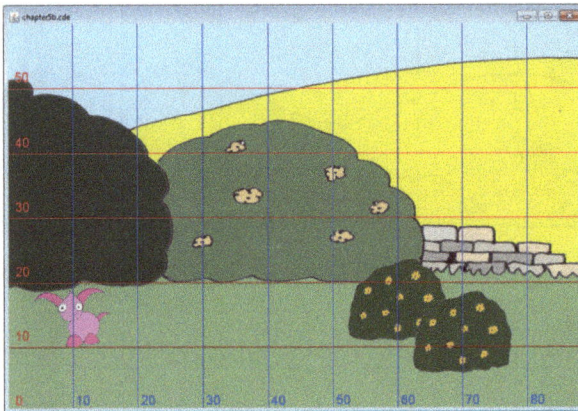

2. Now add Drax, but put him outside the scene to the left and near the top so he will fly in above the bushes.

add(drax,-20,40);

3. Make Drax fly into the centre of the scene while Pip does nothing. (Perhaps she is frozen with fear).

3

4. Make Pip run to the right and hide behind the bushes. Drax just looks on.

4 ▶

5. Now get Drax to fly out of the scene to the right, while Pip waits till he has gone before she leaves the scene on the left.

5 ▶

Save

Playing around

Load | File > Open > chapter5c.cde

Here we are going to create a lily-pond and then add Pip and Flup into the scene and get them to leap from lily to lily.

1. Add some flowers in the lake and add in Pip and Flup at a good spot. Here's one I designed. Also tell them both to **rest** for a while.

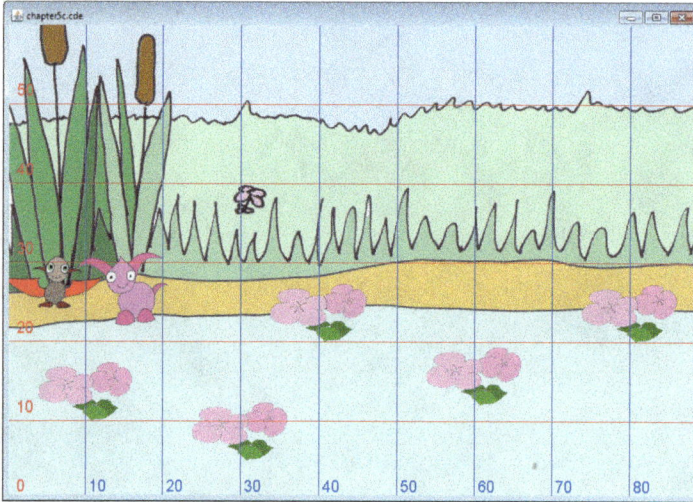

2. Now add the following code to get them both to leap to a different lily, at the same time. Your coordinates may be different from mine.

```
pip.leapto(10,10);
flup.leapto(30,5);
pip.rest();
flup.rest();
```

3. Now add four lines of code to do the following. Pip leaps to another lily while Flup stays still. **Then** Flup leaps to a lily while pip stays still.

4. Now add four lines of code to get both Pip and Flup to rest a while, and then to leap to the same lily at the same time.

5. Now add code to get both Pip and Flup to rest a while, and then fly out of the scene together.

Save

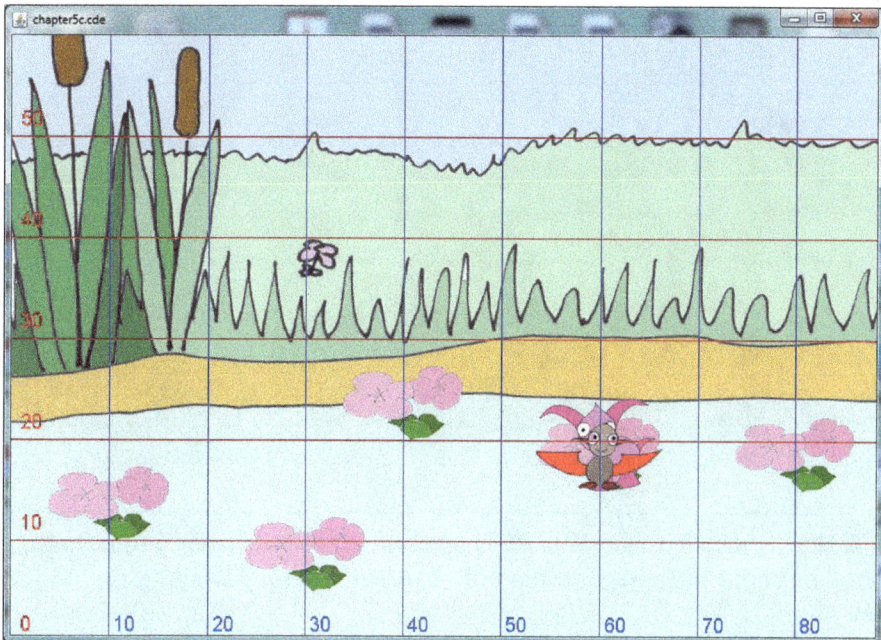

Coming Together

Load   File > Open > chapter5d.cde

In this short story, Flup and Saff will come together, do a little dance, then fly off somewhere else.

1. Let's start by adding some scenery. Add a rug to the right on the ground, a mushroom to the left, and the sun in the sky. Then place Flup and Saff by the lake, and make them both rest a while. Here is what I did.

2. Now add code to get Flup to fly up close to the sun, while Saff goes to the mushroom. Then get them both to rest there for a while.

3. Now add code to get Flup to go to the rug, **then** get Saff to fly to the rug.

4. Now add code to get both Flup and Saff to jump at the same time, then rest.

5. Finally, add code to get Flup to fly off out of the scene, **then** to get Saff to fly out of the scene.

Save

Answers to Some questions

Here are the answers to the labelled questions (numbered yellow circles)

---

1.   **pip.jump();**
           mop.rest();

           mop.jump();
           pip.rest();

---

2.   **mop.flyto(100,50);**
           pip.rest();

---

3.   **drax.flyto(40,40);**
           pip.rest();

---

4.   **pip.runto(65);**
           drax.rest();

---

5.   **drax.flyto(100,55);**
           pip.rest();

           pip.flyto(-20,10);
           drax.rest();

6

Talking, Thinking, and Feeling

Expressing personality

Our characters may want to have conversations, so here we are going to learn how to get them to speak. Characters should also be able to think about things, so we shall learn how to do that. Finally we shall see how they can express emotions. This will help us to develop the individual character, and also with how they interact with other characters.

A Conversation

Load

File > Open > chapter6a.cde

1. Add two characters into the scene and ask them both to rest for a while. I shall choose Pip and Drax.

2. Add the following code to get Pip to say something to Drax, while Drax listens on.

pip.says("Hello Drax");
drax.rest();

3. Of course, Drax will reply, so type the following.

drax.says("Hi Pip, what have you been up to?");
pip.rest();

4. Then Pip will reply. Perhaps she will start to tell a story?

pip.says("I went up into the hills to look for Grog");
drax.rest();

We see there is a ***pattern*** in coding a conversation. Each statement of speech and a response needs 4 lines of code, for example,

pip.says("Some statement");
drax.rest();
drax.says("A reply to pip");
pip.rest();

5. Use this *pattern* to continue the conversation between Pip and Drax. Make sure the conversation comes to a good ending.

Save

Giving Instructions

Speech is often used to ask someone to do something. It could be a movie director telling their actors how to move on the set. Here we shall explore how one character gives instructions and how a second character responds. In the activity below, Flup has got a job as a director, and he is telling Mop how to act. You will see Flup at the bottom-left of the stage, ready to direct his actor, Mop, who is waiting out of sight on the left. The scene, including adding Mop and Flup, has already been set up by the line setStage(); which is inside the engine.

| Load | File > Open > chapter6b.cde | |

1. The director tells Mop what to do. Add the following code.
   ```
   flup.says("Mop , go to centre stage");
   mop.rest();
   ```

2. Write code to get Mop to respond. Don't forget to make Flup rest.

3. The director gives another instruction.
   ```
   flup.says("Now , jump twice");
   mop.rest();
   ```

4. Write code to get Mop to respond. Don't forget to make Flup rest.

5. The director gives another instruction.

flup.says("Now move to the front of the stage");
mop.rest();

6. Write code to get Mop to respond. Don't forget to make Flup rest.

7. Then Mop has to say her lines. She reads her script and says

mop.says("Mary had a little lamb");
flup.rest();
mop.rest();
flup.rest();

8. Add more groups of four lines to complete a script

9. Now give directions to Mop to leave the stage, and make Mop leave the stage.

Save

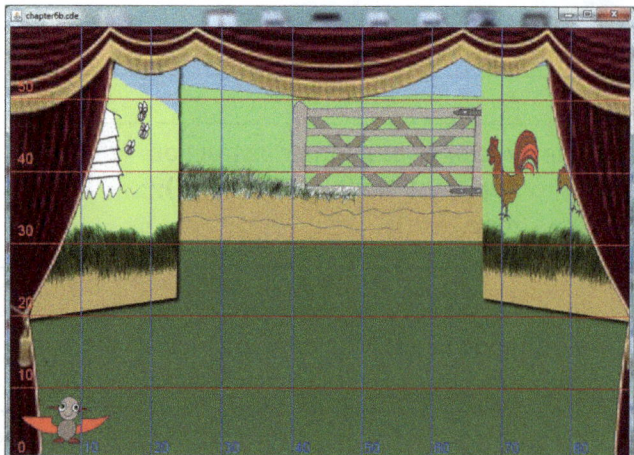

Thinking

Thinking is a bit like talking to yourself; like speaking your thoughts inside your head. In a story, when a character expresses a thought, it is communicating something to the reader, and not to other characters in the story. So that's the real difference between thinking and speaking in the engine. Use thinking to talk to the reader, and speaking to talk to other characters. Of course, it's not quite as simple as that, but it is a start.

Load	File > Open > chapter6c.cde	▶

1. The alien Zon is looking around and he sees something rather strange. He starts thinking. Add the following code.

```
zon.thinks("I wonder what will happen next?");
zon.rest();
```

2. Now add two lines of code where he answers his own question as a thought. Imagine what might happen.

3. Now get Zon to express one more thought.

Save

Showing Emotions

All characters can show several emotions. This is important when you are developing your character. Pip may become scared when she sees Drax the dragon. Writing this line of code,

pip.feels(scared);

will change her face so that she looks scared. Here is the list of emotion words you can use, like in the example above.

---

content, happy, puzzled, sad, excited,

scared, worried, angry, surprised

Load	File > Open > chapter6d.cde	▶

1. Add Pip near the lake, and get her to move to the right of the scene and rest a while.

2. Now add Drax off-screen to the left, then get him to fly in and hover above Pip. (Don't forget to make Pip rest).

3. Now Pip becomes scared (she thinks Drax is bad, and she does not see his smile).

```
pip.feels(scared);
drax.rest():
```

4. But Drax is not bad at all, in fact he is a very friendly dragon, at least on Tuesdays, and today is Tuesday. So Drax tells Pip that he wants to become a friend.

> **drax.says("Pip, do not be scared. I want to be your friend");**
> **pip.rest();**

5. Pip now feels better, so get her to change her emotion to something positive. (Don't forget to make Drax rest).

6. Code a short conversation between Pip and Drax where they agree to be friends.

7. Now get both characters to fly off to the same place out of the screen e.g. (100,20) so it will look as though they are meeting up.

Save

7

Working with Props

Things for Characters to use

Props are inanimate objects; unlike characters they are not alive. So they cannot show emotions, speak, or think. But they can move, change size, appear, and disappear. So they can use all the other methods available. Props look like scenery, so to remind you that something is a prop, its name starts with 'my'. For example, **saucer** is scenery, **mysaucer** is a prop. Also, like characters, you can only place one of any type of prop into the scene.

	mysaucer		mymushroom
	myrobin		mybush
	myant		myfire
	myrock		mykite
	myscarecrow		myrug
	mystar		myegg
	myshell		mylog
			mysun
	mytree		mybarrel

Flying Saucer

Load

File > Open > chapter7a.cde

1. Add **mysaucer** onto the surface of the moon, near the bottom left of the scene, and make it rest a while.

2. Add the following code to make mysaucer fly away into space.
```
mysaucer.flyto3D(70,50);
mysaucer.rest();
```

3. Now add some more code to make mysaucer fly around the scene.

Save

Picking up and Putting down

Load

File > Open > chapter7b.cde

1. Write the following code to get Pip to fly to myegg.

pip.flyto(myegg);

Notice how we used the name myegg and not the coordinates.
Characters can flyto props directly.

2. Now get Pip to pick up myegg,

pip.pickup(myegg);

then fly back to her starting point,

pip.flyto(10,10);

then put down myegg,

pip.putdown(myegg);

and then move a little.

pip.stepto(24);

Save

The Collectors

| Load | File > Open > chapter7c.cde | ▶ |

In this scene Pip and Flup are collectors. They roam around the scene picking up props and taking them back to their home. Remember, the characters can only pick up one prop at a time. Also remember, since you have two characters in the scene, then you must code in pairs of lines. Also remember to flyto a prop, instead of using coordinates, like this **pip.flyto(myscarecrow);**

1. At line 18, write code to get Pip to pick up myscarecrow and take it back to her home and put it down there. Flup stays at rest. ▶

2. Write code to get Flup to pick up mymushroom and take it to her home and put it down there. Pip stays at rest. ▶

3. Now write code to get Flup and Pip to collect the two remaining props. ▶

4. Choose two more props and add these into the scene. Do this after the add statements already in the program at line 17. Now get Flup and Pip to collect these two props at the end of the code. ▶

Save

8

Some Simple Stories

Examples from Year 4 (3rd Grade)

Here you are going to code some simple stories. You will be given instructions telling you what to do, but you must choose the code yourself. All of the stories will involve either two characters, or one character and a prop. So you will have to code in pairs of lines. I will suggest particular characters, but you are free to choose your own.

A Night Scene

Load

File > Open > chapter8a.cde

Here we are going to tell the story of Pip meeting a flying saucer.

1. Add **mysaucer** outside the scene to the left.
   Add Pip somewhere on the ground.

2. Now make mysaucer fly across the scene and out at the right while Pip feels scared (at the same time).

3. Now make mysaucer fly back across the scene to the left while Pip remains motionless – she is scared.

4. Now get Pip to fly out of the scene looking for mysaucer.

5. Finally, get both Pip and mysaucer to fly across the scene and exit at the right.

Save

A Camping Trip

| Load | File > Open > chapter8b.cde | ▶ |

1. Write some code to complete this campfire scene. Make sure the characters are sitting on the rug. ▶

2. They are having fun, so make one jump and then the other. Remember to code in pairs, you will need 4 lines! ▶

3. Now add code to make **myegg** appear near the tree-trunk on the right. ▶

4. Flup says, "I will get us some supper," while Pip listens. ▶

5. Flup flies to myegg and picks it up. Pip watches.

6. Then Flup flies to the fire and puts myegg down.

7. Then she goes back to the rug.

8. Pip and Flup jump together while myegg is cooking.

Save

Terror on the Moon

Load

File > Open > chapter8c.cde

Let's code a short story about terror on the Moon. Pip is visiting a friend who lives on the moon. But the horrible dragon Drax appears and makes Pip feel really scared. Suddenly a flying saucer swoops overhead which scares Drax. Let's see what happens.

1. Make Drax move closer to Pip. She feels scared.

2. So Pip moves away from Drax, while he stays still.

3. Drax moves closer to Pip again, but she moves away.

4. A flying saucer (**mysaucer**) appears at the top-left of the scene.

5. It flies across the screen. Drax feels scared and Pip is frozen with fright. ***HINT:*** *You have two actors and a prop in the code now, so you must code in* **triples** *of lines, one for Pip, one for Drax, and one for mysaucer.*

6. Both Drax and Pip get out of the scene as fast as they can.

Save

A Jumping Game

Load

File > Open > chapter8d.cde

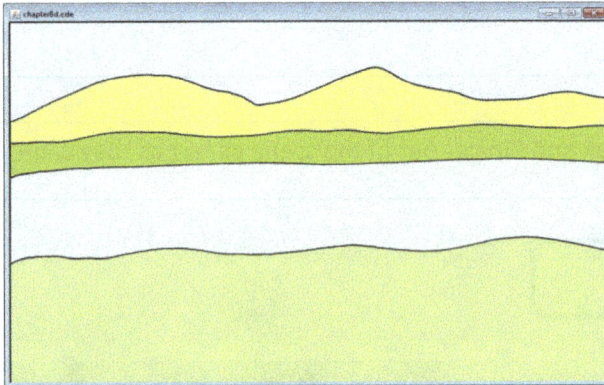

Two characters are going to have a 'jumping' game. This could be either jumping up and down, or jumping over an obstacle. Or you could think of something else.

1. Add some scenery to make this scene more interesting, and also add something to jump over. How about a stack of barrels, or the log? You could even add some fire.

2. Now add two characters and get them to do a series of jumps . Here's a reminder of the choices. I'll use Mop.

mop.jump(30);	Jumps up with height of 30
mop.hopto(50);	Goes over an object, lands at 50
mop.leapto(60,40);	Goes over object, lands at (60,40)

Of course, you could use a longlist of **flyto.**

Save

9

Scene Management

Organizing your code

Stories usually have several scenes or chapters. Here we shall see how to organize a long story into a number of scenes. We shall need to change the background, and remove scenery when we move from scene1 to scene2. Also, a story may need a large number of lines of code. So it is better to group the code for each scene together. This is the first thing we shall explore. Let's look at this code.

```
public void once() {
        scene1();
        scene2();
}

public void scene1() {
        setScene("Lake1");
        add(mushroom,20,10);
        add(pip,30,10);
        pip.jump();
}

public void scene2() {
        changeScene("Lake2");
        add(shell,20,10);
}
```

The first thing we notice, is that there is none of the usual code in the **once()** method. Instead code is placed in the methods **scene1()** and **scene2()**. When the engine runs **once()** then it sees the 'call' to scene1() and jumps there and runs all the code there. When that's done the engine jumps back to **once()** and then sees the call to **scene2()** so it jumps there and runs this code. So all we have to do is to put code for each part of our story (scene) into its own method, and call this in **once().**

Looking at the method **scene1()** we see the familiar **setScene** call to change the background to Lake1. Then we add a mushroom and Pip and then Pip has a jump. That's the end of the first scene.

Looking at the method **scene2()** the first thing we do is to change the background to Lake2. The method **changeScene(...);** first removes previous scenery (the mushroom) and then changes the background. Then the new scenery (the shell) is added.

Characters cannot be deleted from the story. There are two things you can do. First you can hide the character. Second, you can move it out of the scene. In both cases you can then forget about it.

Simple Scene Change

Load | **File > Open > chapter9a.cde**

When you run the code you will see Lake1 with a mushroom and Pip will jump. Then the scene will change to Lake2, the mushroom will have gone and a shell will appear.

1. Add some more scenery to **scene1()** before Pip is added.

2. Now add some more scenery to **scene2()**

3. Add the following lines of code at the end of **scene1()** to get rid of Pip.
    pip.rest();
    pip.hide();

4. Now add more scenery and another character to both scenes. Remember to add the scenery in before you add the characters.

Save

Story with Three Scenes

| Load | File > Open > chapter9b.cde | ▶ |

Here we are going to create a story with three scenes. You could make a plan. A good place to start is to choose the background for each scene, the scenery you want for each scene, and then the characters that fit in best. That's one way.

Another way is not to plan anything, but to start on scene1, work out a bit of a story, and see what happens. This could give you inspiration for your scene2, and then scene2 would give you inspiration for scene3. Then the story is not planned but *emerges*.

1. The code is a *template,* giving you a basic structure to add in your story code. There are two scenes. Add more template code, to extend this to three scenes (you can use copy and paste). Do not add scenes 2 or 3 to the **once()** section until you have designed each scene, otherwise you won't be able to see what you are doing.

2. Now code scene 1. Remember to **hide** characters if you do not want them in a later scene. When you have finished scene 1, you can add **scene2();** in the **once()** section. Now you can code scene 2. Remember to use **changeScene(...)** to remove scenery from scene 1. When you have finished scene 2, you can add **scene3();** to the **once()** section. Now you can code scene 3.

| Save |

10

Adding your own Assets

Being Creative

Our work so far has used built-in backgrounds, scenery, characters and props. In this chapter we shall find out how to add our own. It's quite straightforward really, we need to create our own images and place these in the engine. These have to be deposited in the **data** folder so that you can find them as shown below.

    code
    data   ←
    jre7
    logs
    sounds
    Compiland.class
    Compiland.java
    Header.bak
    Header.txt
    RUN_ME.bat
    template.txt
    WBEngine.jar

Backgrounds

This is easy. All you need is an image 900 pixels wide and 600 pixels high. It should be .jpg format (JPEG image). If you look in the data folder you will find **Anneke.jpg**. Right-click on this and select **Properties** then the **Details** tab. This will show you the size and that the image is a JPEG. You can create your image directly using Photoshop or other editing software, or you can draw your own image on paper and use a scanner or camera to create a digital image. Put your JPEG background into the data folder.

Scenery

This is also quite easy. You will need to create an image of type PNG with a transparent background. Use Photoshop or other editing software. What about the size? The best thing to do is to look at some examples in the **data** folder.

For example look at the **AfricanViolet.png** Right-click and select Properties > Details and you will see the size is 57 pixels wide by 60 pixels high. The bigtree (Tree2.png) has size 443 wide by 500 high. Remember to put your PNG scenery into the data folder.

Props

These are also PNG transparent images, so the same instructions apply as for scenery. However, to use them, we must write two lines of code to get them into our story. Look at the code snippet below.

```
SceneObject  myBubble;

public void once() {
    myBubble = new SceneObject(canvas,"Bubble1");
    add(myBubble,10,10);
    myBubble.flyto(30,50);


}
```

In the first line we choose a name for our prop, I have chosen **myBubble** but you can choose anything. This line tells the engine that myBubble belongs to the class **SceneObject**. Note this line must be written before the method **once()**.

Then, the line mybubble = new SceneObject(canvas,"Bubble1"); actually creates the prop. The name "Bubble1" is the name of the image file inside the **data** folder. After that, we can use the prop as normal, here I add myBubble then get mybubble to fly to (30,50);

Characters

Here we need several PNG images for our new character. This is because they show emotions. The images must be named correctly. Let's take the example of a frog starting with the base image **frog.png**. We must then create the following images and put everything into the **data** folder.

frogcontent.png	frogsad.png	frogscared.png
frogangry.png	frogworried.png	frogsurprised.png
frogexcited.png	frogpuzzled.png	froghappy.png

Look in the **data** folder and you will find these images waiting for you. Here's how to create and use your new character.

```
WeeBee  myFrog;

public void once() {
    myFrog = new WeeBee(canvas,"frog");
    add(myFrog,40,10);
    myFrog.rest();
    myFrog.feels(excited);
}
```

In the first line we choose a name for our new character, I have chosen **myFrog** but you can choose anything. This line tells the engine that myFrog belongs to the class **WeeBee**. Note this line must be written before the method **once()**. Then, the line myFrog = new WeeBee(canvas,"frog"); actually creates the character. The name "frog" is the name of the base image file inside the **data** folder. After that, we can use the prop as normal; here we add myFrog, then get myFrog to rest, and then display the excited emotion.

Using your own Assets

Load	File > Open > chapter10.cde

Here we are going to pretend you have created a new prop, a bubble, and a new character, a frog. You will be guided how to get these assets into the engine. But first we shall start with a background and some new scenery.

1. Add the following line to load a new background.

```
setScene("Anneke");
```

2. Now let's add our new scenery.

```
add("Seaweed1",40,10);
add("Seaweed1",50,8);
```

3. Now let's add our new prop. First, at the top of the code, before **once()** add the following line.

```
SceneObject myBubble;
```

4. Then inside **once()**, after the adds write this code.

```
myBubble = new SceneObject(canvas,"Bubble1");
add(myBubble,30,10);
myBubble.jump();
```

Save

5. Now let's create and use our new frog character **myFrog**. First we must declare our character's name. Write this under the SceneObject myBubble; line.

WeeBee myFrog;

6. Now inside **once()** create myFrog and add it into the scene.

myFrog = new WeeBee(canvas,"frog");
add(myFrog,20,10);

7. Let's make myFrog feel happy.

myFrog.feels(happy);

8. Now use your new background, scenery, props, and character to tell a short story.

Save

11

Working with Sound

Music and Sound Effects

There are two sorts of sounds that you can add to your animation. First are short sound effects that you can combine with character actions, and second you can add music or songs that play continuously as your animation unfolds. These have to be deposited in the **data** folder which you can find as shown below. The sounds live in the **sounds** folder shown below. You can add your own sound files here; they should be of type **.wav**.

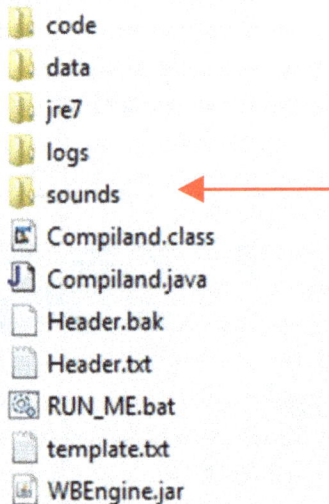

code
data
jre7
logs
sounds ←
Compiland.class
Compiland.java
Header.bak
Header.txt
RUN_ME.bat
template.txt
WBEngine.jar

To play a long sound track such as music, then the following command is used. The whole track will play from start to finish, so the time taken is the length of the track.

mop.sings("song1");

To play a sound effect that lasts for a short time (the same time as a character action), the following method is called.

mop.chirps("sound1");

So in the following lines of code, Mop will make a sound and then jump.

mop.chirps("sound6");
mop.jump();

There is a second way to add a sound effect. Here the sound will play at the same time as the action.

mop.chirps("sound6",true);
mop.jump();

Adding Sound Effects

Load	File > Open > chapter11a.cde

1. Add the following code to play two sound effects separated by some character actions.

```
mop.chirps("sound6");
mop.jump();
mop.chirps("sound4");
mop.jump();
```

2. Now change your code so the sound effects overlap with the actions.

```
mop.chirps("sound6",true);
mop.jump();
mop.chirps("sound4",true);
mop.jump();
```

3. Now add the following code to get a piece of music playing while Mop does some actions

```
mop.sings("greenHill");
mop.jump();
mop.spin();
mop.jump();
```

Save

4. Have a go at recording your own sound effects or finding (or making) some music. Remember the format has to be **.wav** and put your sounds into the **sounds** folder.

12

Story Types and Starters

Ideas for composition

You might find you are coding a story in one of two ways. The first is to write lines of code and let your story emerge. So you write some code, and you look at the animation and this gives you an idea of 'what happens next'. The other way is to plan a story in your head (or at least a story outline) and then code it. Or you may find yourself using a mix of the two. So let's see how each of these approaches works.

Emergent Stories

Stories emerge when scenery, props and characters are put together in meaningful ways. What does this mean? Well think about Drax the dragon and the prop *myFire*; these certainly belong together since it is well-known that dragons breathe fire. The character Zon and the flying saucer *mysaucer* belong together; since Zon is an alien and both these things are about space. In fact, if you look inside *mysaucer* then you will see Zon's twin brother. What about all the other pieces of scenery - the props and characters. How can we work out what belongs with what. I shall explain. This uses the idea that all of these things possess *affordances* - what they can do and what can be done to them. One important affordance is where the thing is usually found (a cloud would be in the sky). Another affordance is what the thing suggests, e.g., fire suggests danger. Let's look at some examples.

Asset	Affordance	Location
	+ can be sat on + magic carpet	+ ground + in the air
	+ danger + cooking	+ ground
	+ flight + space travel	+ sky + space
	+ stand on + hide in	+ ground
	+ friendly + can fly, perch	+ in tree + on fence
	+ hide behind	+ ground
	+ fragile + birth	+ ground + nest
	+ gives light + constellation	+ night sky
	+ female + friendly	+ ground
	+ male + scary	+ anywhere

Planned Stories

You can code a story based on stories you know. Stories can be grouped into 'types', for example Cinderella belongs to the type **Rivalry** because her ugly sisters are rivals for the hand of the Prince. So here we are going to think about story types and give examples of stories you may know.

Storytype Quest

This is a search for a person, or a thing, or a place. You could use many scenes, perhaps ending up in the same scene where you started. Your character should change as a result of the quest, and you should make this clear. A good example is *'Jack and the beanstalk'*.

> *Jack and his mother have fallen on hard times. Jack is searching for a way to feed himself and his mother. At the start of the story, Jack is lazy and sells his mother's cow for a handful of 'magic' beans rather than go to market. By the end of the story Jack shows courage and determination in defeating the giant.*

Storytype Pursuit

Here there is a chase, and the chase is more important than the characters involved. In your story, the pursued character should have a real chance of getting caught. There should be a lot of action (rather than speech or thought). A good example is *'The Gingerbread Man'*.

> *As soon as the gingerbread man is let out of the oven the chase begins. He doesn't want to be eaten but gets chased by everyone he meets and they all want to eat him.*

Storytype Rescue

Here there is a lot of action, which is more important than character development. You should have a hero, a villain, and the victim. The hero rescues the victim from the villain, and your story should focus on the hero's search for the victim and the victim's plight. A good example is *'Little Red Riding Hood'*.

> *Little Red Riding Hood is lured away from the safe path by the wolf who then lays a trap for her at Grandmother's house. Little Red Riding Hood realises that the wolf is in disguise and cries for help. She is rescued at the last minute by the hero woodcutter who hears her cries.*

Storytype Escape

Here there is a lot of action. The hero is imprisoned or confined in some way and wants to escape. The hero is actually the victim. Your first scene deals with the victim's imprisonment, the second could deal with the escape plans, and the third scene deals with the actual escape. A good example is *'The Three Little Pigs'*.

> *Each of the three pigs builds a house. The first two houses are blown down by the wolf and the pigs escape to the third house of bricks. When the wolf arrives at the house of bricks the pigs are trapped inside, but the foolish wolf tries to climb down the chimney and dies.*

Storytype Revenge

Here you have a goodie (protagonist or hero) and a baddie (antagonist). The baddie gives the goodie some sort of injury. You should focus on the build up to revenge or the antagonist getting their just desserts. You should focus on the build up to revenge or the antagonist getting their just desserts.

The opening scene should present the goodie's usual life, and then the baddie interferes with this. In the second scene, the plot develops as the goodie finds safety and the baddie plots further harm. The third scene could be the final confrontation between goodie and baddie, where the baddie actually gets his just desserts. A good example is *'Snow White and the Seven Dwarfs'*.

> *The vain queen is jealous of Snow White's beauty so she arranges for Snow White to be abandoned in the forest at the mercy of wild animals. She finds the seven dwarfs who look after her. The queen finds out from her magic mirror and wants to get rid of Snow White permanently by poisoning an apple. The poisoned apple puts Snow White into a coma until she is found by a prince who saves her. When the wicked Queen finds out she flies into a rage that kills her.*

Storytype Rivalry

This is about the struggle for power between the goodie and the baddie(s). A good example is *Cinderella*. The baddie(s) start off with more power than the goodie, but the goodie has something extra. The first scene should explain the rivalry before the action begins. The second scene could depict how the baddie(s) attack the goodie. The next scenes show how the goodie has a reversal of fortune and the baddie(s) are overcome.

> *The step sisters and step mother force Cinderella to live and work like a servant. But Cinderella is good and kind and takes care of the animals. The step sisters try to stop Cinderella going to the ball even though she has been invited. The animals help Cinderella to get to the ball where the Prince falls in love with her. At the end of the story, Cinderella marries the Prince and the step sisters have gained nothing.*

Storytype Transformation

This is about how the character changes as they progress through a journey. The actions and speech of the character should show how they are changing. In the first scene, the character faces a situation that is going to cause them to change. In the second scene, you should show how the situation actually causes the change, and in the third scene the character should describe the change they have undergone. A good example is *Beauty and the Beast.*

> *At the beginning, the Prince shows himself to be an uncaring selfish man and so he becomes a beast as punishment. When he meets Beauty he begins to change. At first he is selfish and wants to keep her in his castle, but he gradually falls in love with her and that changes him. When her father falls ill, he lets Beauty go not expecting to ever see her again. But Beauty does return and the beast is transformed back into a Prince.*

Storytype Love

There should always be an obstacle to love. Your characters may want it, but they can't have it so easily. The characters should be ill-suited in some way; perhaps they are unequal socially, or perhaps one is handicapped. One character should be seeking love, and the other responding to the seeking. You should aim to show emotions as your story develops. Also, remember that love stories need not have happy endings. A good example is *Rapunzel.*

> *Rapunzel is kept imprisoned in a tower by an evil witch who agreed to let Rapunzel's poor parents have food in exchange for the child. A Prince heard Rapunzel singing and fell in love with her. She was only a peasant's daughter and trapped in a tower by a wicked witch with no means of escape. The Prince tried to rescue her but the witch cut off Rapunzel's hair. The Prince searched for Rapunzel and eventually heard her singing and found her, and they were married.*

Storytype Discovery

This could be about the process of discovery: exploring strange lands, having new experiences, finding a new object or animals. A good example is *Gulliver's Travels*.

> *Gulliver is a sea captain who travels to remote fictional regions of the world. He discovers an island called Lilliput where the people are less than 15 cm tall. He then travels to Brobdingnag where the people are all giants. Next he is captured by pirates and is set adrift and finds himself on an island in the clouds. Finally he visits the land of the Houyhnhnms, a race of intelligent horses. Gulliver returns to England where he finds he prefers horses to people.*

But it could also be about *personal* discovery, where a character gets to know himself through his experiences. A good example is *The Hobbit*.

> *Bilbo Baggins is a simple Hobbit, who at the beginning of the story is timid, quiet, and home loving, living safely in the shire. Just leaving the shire and setting out on adventure required great bravery. During his dangerous adventures he discovers that he is more courageous and clever than he ever would have thought he was.*

What Happens Next?

The images presented below are story-starters. If you ask yourself, 'What happens next?' then this might suggest a short story. In the first starter there is an injured robin up a tree. Pip and Grog look on very frightened. What happens next?

Think about what the fire can do. The robin is injured and cannot fly. But think what Pip or Grog could do.

In the example below, Pip wants to cross a bridge but a Troll pops up. What happens next? What could the Troll do if Pip approaches? What choices of action does Pip have?

Here we can just catch a glimpse of Pip and Grog hiding behind some trees. Are they playing hide and seek? What happens next?

Flup is standing on the top of a stack of barrels. They look a little wobbly. What could happen next?

Each question 'What happens next?' has more than one possible answer (there are no 'correct' answers). Will the barrels tumble? Will Flup fall and will the barrels land on top of him? Or will he fly off? That's your choice, your story.

13

Advanced Coding

Constructs

Our code so far has focused on creating animated stories. In this chapter, we shall turn to more advanced ways of writing code, and we shall introduce some important computing vocabulary (in italics) such as *blocks* of code. What is a code *block*? This is several lines of code that are contained within curly brackets, left curly bracket { at the start, and right curly bracket } at the end. You've seen this already; here the curly brackets are highlighted in green.

```
public void once() {
    add(pip,10,10);
    pip.jump();
}
```

In chapter 10 we saw how to create our own assets. For example, to create a bubble object we wrote **SceneObject myBubble;**
The word **myBubble** is a *variable* which is a place in computer memory.
We created a SceneObject and *assigned it* to the *variable* **myBubble** like this.
myBubble = new SceneObject(canvas,"Bubble1");

We say that the *variable* **myBubble** is an *object* that belongs to the *class* **SceneObject**.

Repetition: **The while-loop**

Often in coding we need to repeat some operation. Suppose we want Pip to jump 5 times. We could write 5 lots of pip.jump(); statements. That would work. But suppose we wanted pip to jump 100 times. Writing 100 lots of pip.jump(); statements is nonsense.

Fortunately, there is a *coding construct* that makes life much easier. This is the *while-loop*. So let's see how this works.

```
1       count = 5;
2       while(count > 0) {
3           pip.jump();
4           count = count – 1;
5       }
6       pip.rest();
```

The first thing to notice are the curly brackets on lines 2 and 5. They enclose a *block* of code - lines 3 and 4. Line 2 is the key; in simple English it says 'if the value of **count** is greater than 0, then run the code *block*. So here's how this code snippet works.

i) Line 1 sets the value of the *variable* **count** to 5.

ii) Line 2 looks at the value of **count**, is it greater (>) than **0**? It is, so run the *block*, lines 3 and 4.

iii) Line 3 makes pip jump.

iv) Line 4 subtracts 1 from the value of **count**. It was 5 so it is now 4.

v) We have reached the end of the code *block* (curly bracket, line 5) so we go back to the start of the *block* (line 2).

vi) Is **count** (4) greater than zero? Yes, so { Pip jumps again, and **count** goes down to 3 }

You get the idea. The *while-loop* counts down, 5,4,3,2,1, and when it reaches 0 the *block* of code is finished, and the next line of code to be *executed* is line 6. Pip has deserved a well-earned rest.

A Loopy Jump

Here we shall explore the *while loop* discussed above. I shall use Pip (you have probably guessed she's one of my favourite WeeBees); you can choose your own character.

Load	File > Open > chapter13a.cde	▶

1. Look at the code. You will see the new character **myFrog** is used. It is *declared* at the top of the code. Also you will see the line **int count;** This is *declaring* the *variable* **count**. It tells us that the *type* of the *variable* is **int** which is short for *integer*. An integer is a whole number, -2, -1, 0, 1, 2, 3, ...

2. Now underneath the line where myFrog is added, set the value of **count** to a number.

count = 5;

3. Now build up the *while loop.* Use the tab key for extra indentations.

```
while(count > 0) {
    myFrog.jump();
    count = count - 1;
}
```

4. After the bottom curly bracket, on the next line, get myFrog to spin.

myFrog.spin();

Save

Adding Comments

It is useful to add comments into code to remind us what the code does. We can get a character to speak comments to us, to tell us where we are in the code, and to tell us the value of a *variable.* Here's how **myFrog** will tell us the value of count.

myFrog.says("Count is " + count);

5. Add the following line just before the **while(...** statement.
   myFrog.says("At the start of the while loop");

6. Add the following line inside the while loop just after **myFrog** does his jump.
   myFrog.says("In while-loop. Count is " + count);

7. Now add the following at the end of the while loop, after the curly bracket } on the next line.
   myFrog.says("While loop finished. Count is " + count);

8. Now change the code so that **myFrog** jumps 10 times.

Save

SaveAs

File > SaveAs > chapter13b

More Fun with Loops

Here we shall use the loop counter **count** to change the jump height of myFrog.

Load	File > Open > chapter13b.cde	▶

1. At the top of the program, *declare* another *variable* of *type integer* like this:

int height;

We shall use this to change the jump height of myFrog.

2. We shall calculate the height from the value of count. Let's agree to make the height 10 times the count. Put the following line of code before the instruction myFrog.jump();

height = 10*count;

3. Now change the code that makes myFrog jump, to use the value of the *variable* **height**.

myFrog.jump(height);

4. Now get myFrog to tell you the height when he jumps instead of the count.

5. Change the code to get all the jumps higher.

Save

Selection

So far our code has worked from start to end as though we are walking along a straight path. But sometimes we need to get our code to make a choice; to turn left or right when the path has a branch or fork. When myFrog is in a loop and makes 6 movements, then we may want the first 4 to be jumps and the last 2 to be spins. To do this we use the *selection construct*. Here's how we code this example.

```
if (count > 2)
        myFrog.jump();
else
        myFrog.spin();
```

What is happening here? Well remember that the value of **count** is changing in the loop. So this construct says, in simple English, "If the value of count is greater than 2, then myFrog jumps, else if it is not then myFrog spins".

How does this work? Suppose that **count** starts at 6, then it goes 6,5,4,3,2,1,0. So for the first four jumps it is 6,5,4,3. These values are all greater than 2 (> 2), so this is the *condition* we use in the if-statement **if(count > 2)**.

| Load | File > Open > chapter13c.cde | ▶ |

1. Add the following lines inside the while-loop after the statement **height = 10*count;**

```
if( count > 2 )
    myFrog.jump(height);
else
    myFrog.spin()
```

2. Run your code and check that myFrog jumps 4 times and spins twice.

▶

3. Change your code to make myFrog jump 3 times and then spin 3 times.

▶

4. Change the code to make myFrog jump 6 times and then spin 4 times.

▶

5. Change the code to do the opposite, make myFrog spin 6 times and then jump 4 times.

▶

| Save |

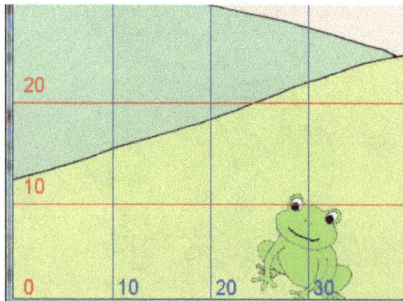

Selection of Blocks

Here we shall use the *selection construct* to work with *blocks* of code, to choose which *block* will run.

Load	File > Open > chapter13c.cde	▶

1. Change your *selection construct*, adding curly brackets { } so that your code looks like this:

```
if( count > 2 ){
    myFrog.jump(height);
    myFrog.says("I've jumped");
} else {
    myFrog.spin();
    myFrog.says("I've spun");
}
```

Save

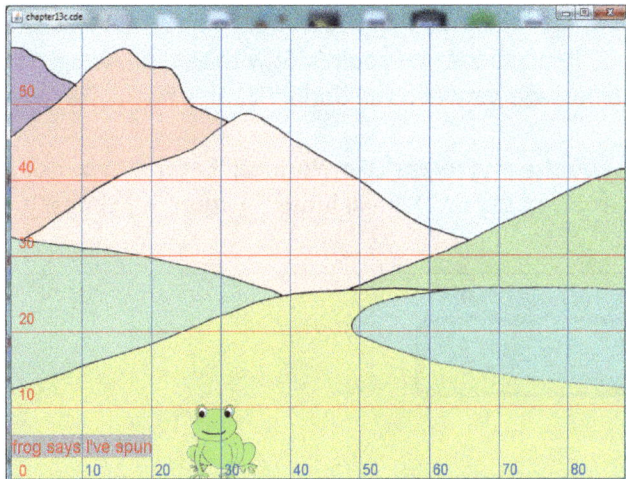

User Input

Getting input from the user can change the way a program runs. We can ask the user to tell us how many jumps to make, how high to jump, or how fast to spin. We can also ask the user to select between several scenes in a story. How to ask for user input is shown below. The words in speech marks will appear on the canvas. The word on the left is the *variable* that receives the input value.

count = myFrog.asksForNumInt("Enter number of jumps");

Here is what the user will see, where she had entered 5.

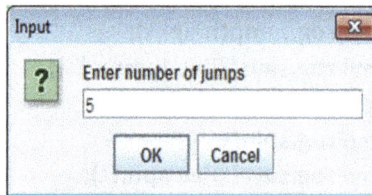

| Load | **File > Open > chapter13d.cde** | ▶ |

1. Replace the line **count = 5;** with the following. You can change the message between the double quotes if you like.

count = myFrog.asksForNumInt("Enter number of jumps");
myFrog.says("OK I will jump " + count + " times");

| Save |

Another Loop Structure

The loops presented so far have involved 'counting down' from a starting number. A loop can work by starting at 0 and counting up, like this one.

```
count = 0;
while( count < 5 ){
    myFrog.jump();
    count = count + 1;
}
```

Here the *while loop* code *block* is run while count is less than 5. So the value of count will be 0, 1, 2, 3, 4. You see the loop has run 5 times.

Load	File > Open > chapter13e.cde	▶

1. Type in the following code to create a forest of 5 trees.

```
count = 0;
while( count < 5 ) {
    location = 10*count;
    add(tree,location,10);
    count = count + 1;
}
```

2. Change the code to add 7 trees.

3. Change the location calculation to this.

```
location = 15 + 10*count
```

Save

14

WeeBee Engine Assets

Scenery, Backgrounds, Props and Characters

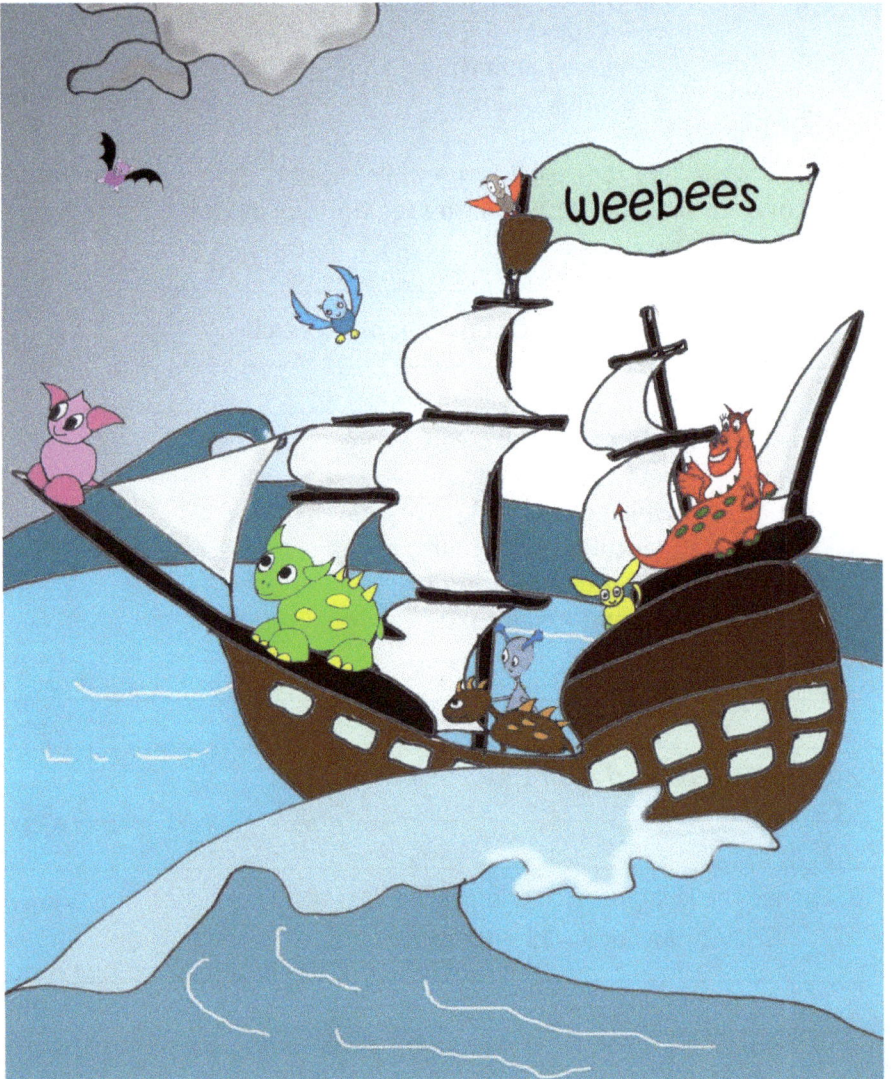

Scenery

ant	mushroom
barrel	rock
rush	rug
bush	saucer
cloud	scarecrow
dandelion	shell
egg	star
fire	sun
flower	sunflower
kite	bigtree
storm	tree
log	robin

Props

 mysaucer

 myrobin

 myant

 myrock

myscarecrow

mystar

myshell

mytree

mymushroom

myrabbit

 mybush

 myfire

mykite

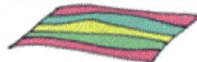 myrug

myegg

 mylog

 mysun

mybarrel

 myship

Characters

Pip

Zon

Grog

Saff

Jig

Mop

Flup

Tod

Drax

List of functions available (on left) with examples and explanations

move-at		
jump(height)	pip.jump(10);	Pip jumps up 10 units
spin(speed)	pip.spin(5);	Pip spins with speed = 5 (slow)
flipH()	pip.flipH();	Pip does about-face
hide()	pip.hide();	Pip hides out of sight
show()	pip.show();	Pip reappears after hiding
grow(scale)	pip.grow(1.5);	Pip grows by half (0.5) of usual size
shrink(scale)	pip.shrink(0.5);	Pip shrinks by half (0.5) of usual size
rest()	pip.rest();	Pip does nothing

move-to		
flyto(X,Y);	pip.flyto(60,30);	Pip moves to coordinates (60,30)
flyto(prop);	pip.flyto(myrug);	Pip moves to myrug
flyto3D(X,Y);	grog.flyto3D(60,40);	Grog moves into the distance
leapto(X,Y)	pip.leapto(60,30);	Pip leaps to (60,30)
walkto(X)	pip.walkto(60);	Pip walks to X = 60;
runto(X)	pip.runto(60);	Pip runs to X = 60;
hopto(X)	pip.hopto(60);	Pip hops to X = 60;
flapto(X)	jig.flapto(50);	Jig goes to X = 50, wings flapping
stepto(X)	pip.stepto(50);	Pip goes to X = 50, legs moving

Speaking, Singing and Thinking		
says("words");	pip.says("Hello");	
chirps("soundfile");	pip.chirps("sound1.wav");	Sounds are in the
sings("soundfile");	pip.sings("tune1.wav");	'sounds' folder
thinks("words");	pip.thinks("Drax is scary");	

Possession		
pickup(prop);	pip.pickup(myant);	My ant hides, moves with Pip
putdown(prop);	pip.putdown(myant);	then reappears

Emotions		
feels(emotion)	pip.feels(excited);	

Scene Management		
add(scenery,X,Y);	add(tree,20,10);	
add(scenery,X,Y,front);	add(tree,20,10,front);	Character move behind
add(character,X,Y);	add(pip,40,10);	
setScene("filename");	setScene("forest");	New background
changeScene("filename);	changeScene("forest");	Clear scenery first

15

What you will find in the next book

Turtle Graphics

This book has been all about Story-Writing-Coding. The next book is entirely different. Here we shall explore "Turtle Graphics". The turtle is a little critter that you can instruct to move forwards and turn left and right. You can also tell it to draw a coloured line. The picture below shows a single turtle starting to draw some stairs.

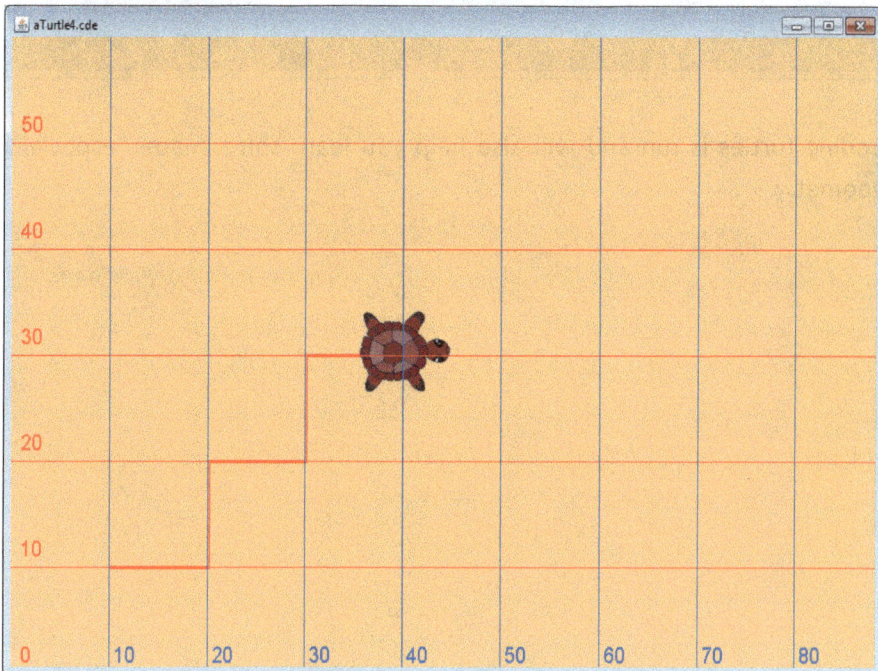

In this example two turtles have collaborated to draw a house.

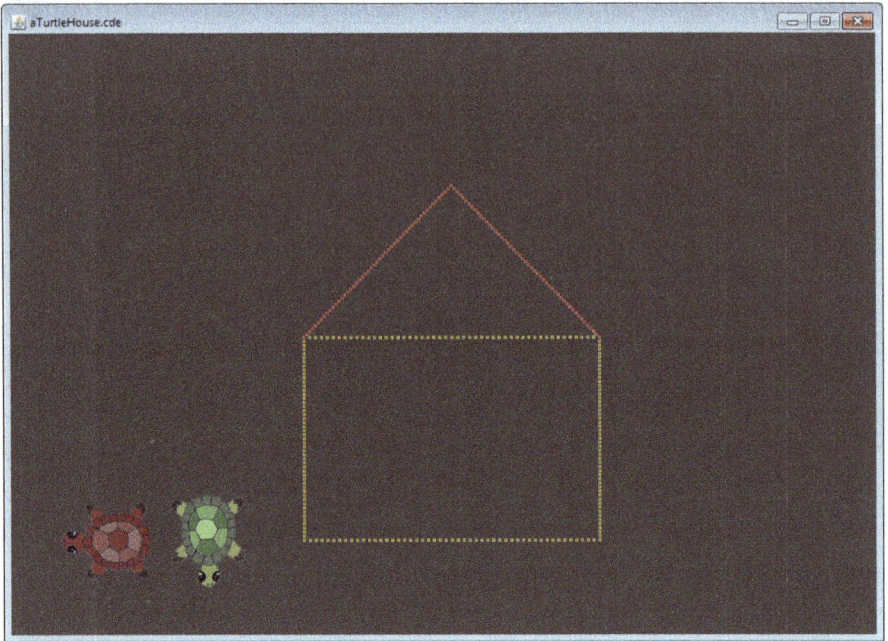

Coding turtles is fun and will also help you learn some maths, especially geometry.

16

Code Index

Where you can find examples of code

Here is a list of code statements and some page numbers where they are used. The first number in **bold** is the first occurrence. Code starting with a dot refers to methods that props and/or characters can use, for example **.jump();** could be used by Pip like this **pip.jump();**

add(scenery,X,Y);	**p5**, p9, p10, p51
add(character,X,Y);	**p5**, p18, p20, p21
add(scenery,X,Y,front)	**p10**
changeScene("background")	**p51**
chirps(filename)	**p61**, p62
feels(emotion)	**p38**, p59
flapto(X)	**p21**
flip(H)	**p15**
flyto(X,Y)	**p5**, p9, p14, p15
flyto(prop)	**p42**
flyto3D(X,Y)	**p5**, p17, p19, p41
grow(scale)	**p15**

hide()   **p15**

hopto(X)   **p20**, p24, p50

jump()   **p14**, p24, p32

jump(height)   **p14**,p50

leapto(X,Y)   **p17**, p18, p28, p50

pickup(prop)   **p42**

putdown(prop)   **p42**

rest()   **p5**, p9, p14, p15

runto(X)   **p20**, p32

says("words")   **p34**, p35, p36, p39

setScene("background")   **p9**, p51, p56, p58

show()   **p15**

shrink(scale)   **p15**

sings(filename)   **p60,** p62

spin()   **p14**

spin(speed)   **p14**

stepto(X)   **p21**, p42

thinks("words")   **p37**

walkto(X)   **p20**